Textiles
As Art

Textiles As Art

Hotel designed by Skidmore, Owings & Merrill, Chicago
Lucien Lagrange, Senior Designer

Tapestry by Sheila Hicks at entrance of a hotel.

Room and furniture designed by James Olson, Olson Sundberg Architects, Seattle

Tapestry by Nancy Southers in a residence.

Acknowledgments

Organizations and people who helped the author:

Max Allen
Vern M. Brooks
Canadian Conservation Institute
Nancy Christensen
Dennis R. Dodds
Betty Freudenheim
Jim Glenn
Richard Girvin
Sharon Girvin
Karen E. Gray
Lloyd Herman
Dorothy Hughes
Illuminating Engineering Society
Ruth Jamison
Nobuko Kajitani
Gregory L. Kay
John D. Kuzlik
Dale Lantvit
Jack Lenor Larsen
Santina M. Levey
Jane Merritt
Robert A. McCully
Ontario Museum Association
Terry Olson
Lydia Puccinelli
Robert Pudil
Natalie Rothstein
Murray Schnaper
Constance Shirakawa
Barbara Smith
Leslie Melville Smith
Smithsonian Institution (SITES)
Lidia Solorzano
Rebecca A. T. Stevens
Textile Conservation Centre
Textile Conservation Workshop

Contents

Introduction

1 Part One
Selecting Textile Art

55 Part Two
Framing and Mounting Textile Art

73 Part Three
Positioning Art

81 Part Four
Lighting Art

93 Part Five
Care and Maintenance of Textiles

100 Questions and Answers

104 About the Author

Interior design: Laurie Smith, Laurie Smith Design Associates, Austin, Texas

Turkman pillow cover (left) and Moroccan rug in reception area of an accounting firm.

Introduction

Beyond the enrichment of upholstery, draperies and carpets, textiles can create the ultimate embellishment: Art.

Navajo shoulder blanket, Moki style.

The Allure of Textile Art

Textiles — contemporary, historical and ethnographic — have universal appeal: emotional, visual, tactile and intellectual.

Textiles as <u>art</u> are uniquely effective for decorating a home, an office, a lobby, a bank or a restaurant.

What are the appealing qualities that make textile art useful to designers and decorators?

- Prints and paintings are pictures of objects; textile art is the real object itself — alive, fully exposing its construction, even its imperfections.

- Textile art can add color and festive excitement.

- Textile art can add shapes to offset geometric alignments of furnishings and add textures to offset sleek machine-made furnishings.

- Because textile art can be very large, it can perform architectural functions — such as visually reshaping a room or directing the eye to focal points.

- Textile art made of heavy thick material can help muffle harsh noises — a welcome bonus in restaurants and building lobbies with tile or terrazzo floors.

- Textile art made of lightweight material is easy to transport and to install.

- For the price of a third-rate painting or a second-rate print, a space could be decorated with a first-rate textile of museum quality.

Intellectual Appeal

Woven into each ethnographic textile is the history of a people–its lore, rituals, myths, symbols– a way of life.

First there are questions about method and technique.

- What is an "ikat"?

  A textile woven with pre-dyed thread – usually tie-dyed in bundles of threads, which accounts for the step-like designs in most ikats.

- What is a "batik"?

  A textile with the design "painted" on it – usually with hot wax – before it is dipped into the dye vat. The wax is then boiled out, leaving a white area where the wax was. The entire process is repeated for each color. Batiks, unlike surface-printed fabric, have completely soaked-through color, so that both sides are equally bright.

Then come questions about use and origin. The simplest question unlocks tales of adventure.

- Why do some Navajo rugs look like Oriental rugs?

- Why do the Amish, known for their plain and somber dress, create quilts so luxuriously detailed and colorful?

- Why is each little design different on a Kuba cloth from Zaire?

- How did the town of Paisley in Scotland become known as the source for shawls ("paisley shawls") which were originally designed and made in Kashmir, India, and called "cashmere shawls"?

Answers at the end of the book.

Art management: Dunning Associates, Philadelphia

Eighteenth century English embroidery in reception area of an accounting firm.

Art Consultant: VIART Corporation, New York

American hooked rug in reception area
of an investment firm.

A Preview

Part 1   Selecting Textile Art
Tells how to select textile art for public space,
corporate collections or personal collections.
Gives advice on commissioning. Tells where to
see and buy textile art. Includes a gallery of
high visual impact textiles — contemporary, historical and ethnographic — from American, British and
Canadian collections.

Part 2   Framing and Mounting
Shows how to frame and mount textile art so that
you can do it yourself or tell a professional framer
what you want.

Part 3   Positioning
Reviews the basics of positioning. Tells how to
use textile art to perform architectural and design
functions in large public spaces such as lobbies,
atriums, hotels, airports and shopping centers.

Part 4   Lighting
Lighting is the most neglected requirement for
effective presentation. Part 4 tells which bulbs
and tubes to use to light textile art.

Part 5   Care and Maintenance
Deliberately kept short and 1, 2, 3 specific — yet
every word has been checked and double-checked
by leading museum conservators.

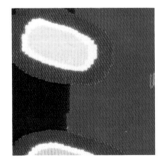

Part One

*How to select for personal collections,
corporate collections and for public space.*

How to commission textile art.

Where to see textile art.

Selecting Textile Art

Selecting for Personal Collections

Building a collection of textile art is almost the same as building a collection of any other kind of art:

- Use experts to help you start.
- Learn as much as you can. See as many different kinds of artwork as you can. Ask questions.
- Buy quality, not quantity.
- Find dealers you can trust and pay the price they ask if you want first choice of new pieces.
- After you buy an artwork, display it and enjoy it.
- Upgrade your collection by selling off, trading and giving away pieces.

What is different about textile art — especially ethnographic textile art — is that good pieces are harder and harder to find. Traditional skills are being lost. In addition, many high-quality textiles have deteriorated because of improper storage and incorrect mounting.

When buying, keep reminding yourself of the age-old advice to collectors: "Buy with your eyes, not your ears!" Cover your ears if a dealer tells you:

"This took six months to make."
"No one knows how this color was made."
"Only the village priest was allowed to make this design."
"Only chiefs could wear this blanket."
"This has brought good luck to everyone who owned it."
"This skirt was danced."

Do not buy any contemporary textile that is:

- A tapestry version of a famous artist's print or painting.
- A tapestry version of a photograph.
- A piece with cute things woven into it.
- A piece that only has meaning after reading its name.
- A piece that is expensive because it is laboriously constructed.

Wise collectors seek pieces in which beauty overlaps importance.

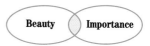

Beauty is determined by the collector's taste and trained eye. Importance is determined by an expert's evaluation of:

Construction details
Condition
Age
Material
Maker/Artist
Rarity

Those who have built valuable collections of any kind of art — with limited funds, educated eye and driving excitement — all knew when beautiful art could also be important art. And they knew before it received the blessing and anointment of the art priests.

Special Considerations for Corporate Collections

Corporate art can decorate the surroundings, support local artists, or give expression to the corporate image. For example, a textile mill might display tapestries, or a clothing manufacturer might display quilts.

Corporate curators should not select artworks with the goal of investing, nor with the goal of educating the employees (a presumptuousness akin to mandating that only Beethoven be played in the employee cafeteria).

Nor should the curator's goal be to excite, arouse or stir controversy. There is no evidence that art-shock stimulates either enlightenment or creativity.

These *caveats* should not scare curators into thinking that their art must fade into the wall. Corporate art can enhance a work place, humanize it, enliven it.

The art need not even blend and match the architecture and furnishings. Some spectacular spaces use "contrapuntal art": art with a tempo and spirit of its own, art that is the opposite of the architecture and furnishings. For example: classic architecture and furnishings decorated with modern art, or sleek modern spaces embellished with old wearing apparel.

Special Considerations for Public Space

No other form of decorative art can so enrich public space as textile art: adding festive decoration, setting human scale, tying together groups of furniture, offering color, texture and human handiwork to soften stark cold walls.

Although using textile art in public spaces has increased, there would be even more if designers allayed client fears. Clients should be told that textile art can survive as long as the building stands if (and they forget to tell the "if") the artwork is constructed of sturdy material, kept out of the sunlight, and mounted so that it can be vacuumed once a year. (If they had a fountain, they would not be shocked to learn that it had to be cleaned at least once a year!)

Architectural design and interior design:
Marshall Erdman and Associates, Inc., Madison, Wisc.

Amish quilts in waiting area of a medical center.

World Bank: Warm, Intimate, Human

The World Bank in Washington, D.C. has transformed its newest building into a warm, intimate and human place to work and to visit. The public areas of the building — hallways, meeting rooms and waiting areas — are decorated with artifacts and textiles from bank-member countries.

Almost all of the textiles are mounted open and uncovered. Very large textiles, such as African dance skirts or caftans, dramatically cover large areas of wall space. Although many are crudely-made and some even ragged, all are authentic and have exciting visual impact.

Sam Niedzviecki, Senior Project Manager of the World Bank, worked with a committee of World Bank employees and museum curators in defining the art program and selecting the pieces.

The selection, purchasing, mounting and positioning were coordinated by Diane Dunning and Liza Sherman of Artco Affiliates, a fine arts management firm based in London, New York and Philadelphia.

There are many kinds of people claiming authority for selecting public space art:

> Architects
> Contractors
> Interior Designers
> Art consultants
> Artists' agents
> Committees of employees
> Museum curators

No one group has proved any more successful than the others. Neither job title nor college degree insures success. Taste and judgment—those twin unmeasurable uncertifiable skills – are still required.

Most textile art in public places fails to meet even the minimum expectation of being appropriate and pleasing. What are the most frequent failures?

- The textile art is too small for the wall. Then to make it worse, it is centered in the middle of the wall!

- The textile art is too high — missing the opportunity for using art to bring down the scale of a high-ceiling space.
  Is it hung high to keep people from touching it? There are better ways to discourage abuse.
  See Part 3 Positioning.

- The textile art is the wrong shape.
  For example: tall vertical art on a long horizontal wall.

- The textile art is the wrong color.
  Example of a mis-match: A dark maroon tapestry on a dark gray wall.... Someone changed the wall color, or someone forgot to ask.

- The textile art is not lit to show it off in a way that enhances the space.
  The price to be paid when the art is a last-minute embellishment and not part of the overall conceptual plan.

- The textile art is unnecessarily covered with glass or plastic which blindingly reflects ceiling lights.
  Typically done in offices, which are the least likely place that the textile would be abused. Covering proclaims to the employees, "We don't trust you!"

Commissioning Textile Art

Appliqued textile art in a residence.

The purpose of commissioning art is to get something unique, something appropriate to the space, something that satisfies the taste of the person paying for it.

To insure that the artist delivers what the commissioner hopes for, it is necessary to explain carefully what is wanted and why; it is then necessary to listen carefully to the artist's counter suggestions or different design concepts.

Before starting a commission, interview the artist, then check-out references from past commissions. (Was the work completed when promised? On budget? Were there any problems with the final artwork that the artist should have forseen?)

To reinforce the understanding, a clear specific written agreement should be made with the artist before work begins. Here is what this written agreement might cover:

- Fees for consultation and design
- Size and materials of the artwork
- Completion schedule
- Payment and payment schedule
  (A frequently used schedule is 50% on approval of design, balance on completion of work.)
- Payment for time and expenses traveling to site of installation
- Responsibility for shipping, insurance, storage and installation
- Copyright ownership
- Responsibility for repair and maintenance

After starting, keep informed of the artist's progress. Keep the artist informed of any changes that could affect the artwork.

When the work is completed and mounted, help the artist obtain exposure and publicity:

- Provide the artist with a professional photograph of the artwork, installed in its setting.
- Have a party to unveil the new art.
- If the art is in a public space, put up a nameplate telling the name of the artist; provide brochures to visitors.
- Show a color photograph of the art in the annual report or employee magazine.
- For a major installation, send out a press release together with a photograph announcing the installation.

Dealing with an artist can be more time-consuming than selecting finished art. However, the patron/artist collaboration – asking, listening, bending, blending – frequently stimulates magnificent creations.

Seeing, Learning About and Buying Textile Art

Courtesy of Malliouhana Hotel, Anguilla   Hotel design: Lawrence Peabody

Indian applique wall hanging in the bar of a hotel.

Contemporary Textile Art

Where to see:

- Craft fairs
- Craft shops
- Art galleries
- Exhibitions

Where to learn more:

- Books and publications in libraries or museum shops
- Photos or slides at crafts councils and at art galleries
- Courses in weaving, quilt-making, surface design, etc.
- Art curators
- Craft curators

Where to buy:

- Craft fairs
- Craft stores
- Art dealers
- Directly from the artists

Ethnographic Textile Art

Where to see:

- Natural history museums
- Art museums
- Textile dealers
- Ethnic arts dealers
- Tribal arts stores
- Trade marts (showrooms featuring imports)

Where to learn more:

- Books and publications from libraries, museum shops, bookstores
- Photos or slides at museum slide libraries
- Travel
- Art consultants
- Museum curators

Where to buy:

- Textile dealers
- Ethnic arts dealers
- Tribal arts stores
- Auctions
- Second-hand stores
- Flea markets

Gallery

The photographs in this section were selected on the basis of:

Visual Impact

The primary consideration is that the textile has high visual impact—a shape, design or color that gives immediate, strong visual delight when seen from across a room.

Personal Familiarity

I have personally seen most of the textiles in this section.

- The Chinese robe, page 50, was selected after opening and inspecting drawer after drawer of robes in the storage room of the Royal Ontario Museum in Toronto.
- The Persian Rugs, pages 13 and 32, Persian saddle cover, page 34, Turkish prayer rug, page 35, and Sumatran ship cloth, page 49, were selected from The Textile Museum in Washington, D.C. I saw them while working there taking inventories, moving storerooms, or helping to mount exhibitions.
- In private homes throughout the United States I have had textile treasures laid in front of me—treasures that any museum would be thrilled to receive.
- Some of the textiles I discovered in remote village markets and bartered for them with facial expressions and sign language.

Office designed and furnishings selected by Mark Hampton, Coconut Grove, Florida

Section of Kuba dance skirt in an office.

A Personal Selection, Not a Survey

No attempt was made to represent each kind of textile or each country or each major collection. No attempt was made to dazzle the eye with unique museum masterpieces.

All of the types of textiles shown in this book are commercially available.

Kimono
Japan
Silk and gold
Embroidered and tie-dyed
c. 1800

Rug (Berber tribe)
Algeria
c. 1930

Tapestry
By Marta Rogoyska
London

Quilt
Lancaster County, Pennsylvania
c. 1860
Appliquéd cotton

◀ **Woven fabric ("Peacock and Dragon")**
Designed by William Morris, England, 1878

Made for drapery and upholstery on a jacquard loom,
in 54″ and 72″ widths (137 and 183cm)

Rug
Persia
19th century

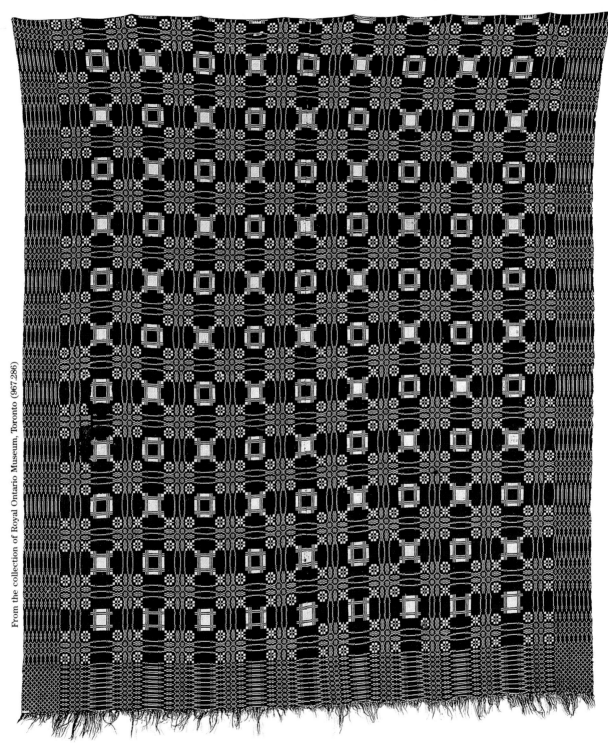

Coverlet
Canada
c. 1850
Woven cotton and wool

Bedding (futon) cover
Japan
Resist-dyed cotton

Poncho
Peru
600-800 AD
Alpaca wool

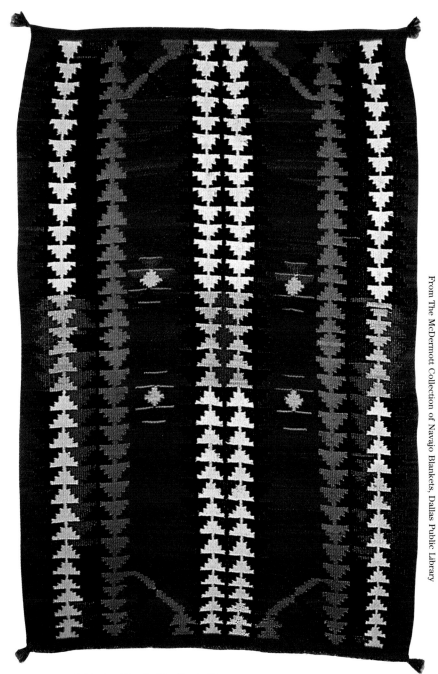

Child's blanket (Navajo "Eye-Dazzler")
U.S.A.
c. 1875
Synthetic-dyed wool

Ceremonial skirt panel (Kuba tribe)
Zaire (Africa)
Appliquéd raffia

Jacket (**suo**)
Japan
c. 1720
Wax-resist dyed linen

Quilt
Hawaii, U.S.A.
c. 1900
Appliquéd cotton

Throne dais carpet (fragment)
China
16th or 17th century
Silk velvet brocade

Bed cover
Uzbekistan, (U.S.S.R.)
18th-19th century
Embroidered (suzani) silk on cotton

Robe (woman's)
Japan
c. 1900
Appliquéd and embroidered cotton

Rug
American
c. 1930
Braided cotton and wool

Wall hanging
By Olga de Amaral
Bogota, Colombia
1985
Woven wool and horsehair, plus gold leaf

Courtesy of Anna and Marianne Yoors, New York

Tapestry
By Jan Yoors
New York
1977

Quilt (Amish "Double Nine")
Lancaster County, Pennsylvania
c. 1910-20

Carrying cloth
Sumatra (Indonesia)
Silk and gold
c. 1890

Rug
Persia
Late 19th century
Slit-tapestry weave (kilim)

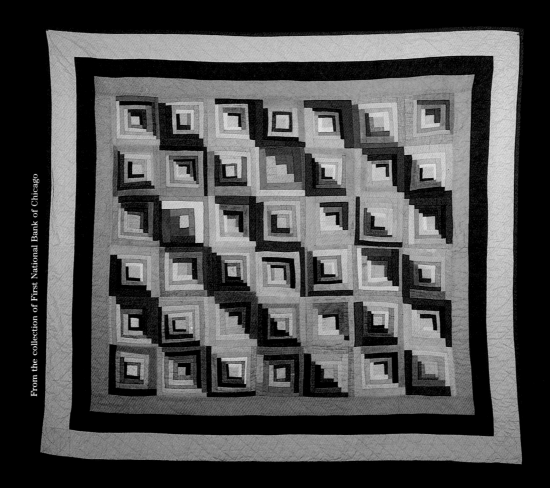

From the collection of First National Bank of Chicago

Crib Quilt (Amish "Streaks of Lightning")
U.S.A.
c. 1930

Rug (sawtooth meander)
Turkey
19th century

Rug
Persia
Late 19th century

Tapestry
By Joanne Soroka
Edinburgh, Scotland
1982

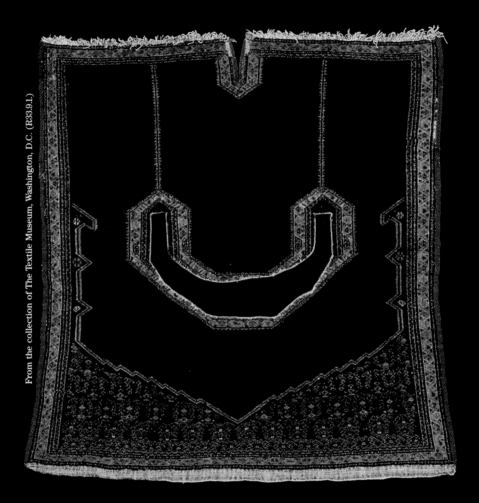

From the collection of The Textile Museum, Washington, D.C. (R33.9.L)

Saddle cover
Persia
Late 19th century
Cotton and wool

From the collection of The Textile Museum, Washington, D.C. (R34.28.5)

Rug
Turkey
19th century
Kilim weave

Banner
By Norman Laliberté
Nahant, Massachusetts
1977
Appliquéd cotton
2½′ × 8′ (76 × 240cm)

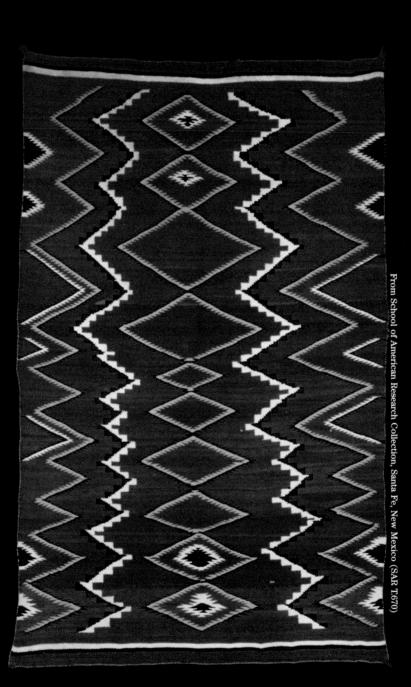

From School of American Research Collection, Santa Fe, New Mexico (SAR T.670)

Blanket (Navajo)
U.S.A.
1870-1885

Chilkat (blanket)
Northwest Indian, Canada
Pre-1876
Wool
5′2″ × 4′4″ (1.58 × 1.32m)

Tapestry
By Lynne Curran
Brampton, Cumbria, England
1984

From the collection of David Pottinger

Quilt (**Amish "Baskets"**)
Made by Mrs. Jacob J. (Fannie) Lambright
U.S.A.
1936

Prayer cloth
Pakistan
Mid-20th century
Cotton, with rayon embroidery
15¾″ × 17″ (40 × 43cm)

Blanket (**Navajo, third phase chief's**)
U.S.A.
c. 1885

Courtesy of Clive Rogers Oriental Rugs, London

Rug
Kazakstan (U.S.S.R.)
Early 20th century
Appliquéd felt

Quilt
Designed and pieced by Charles Cater,
quilted by Willia Ette Graham,
both of Oakland, California.
1986

Courtesy of Martin and Ullman Artweave Textile Gallery, New York

Poncho
Peru (Nazca culture)
100-300 AD
Wool

From the collection of Inger McCabe Elliott, China Seas, Inc., New York

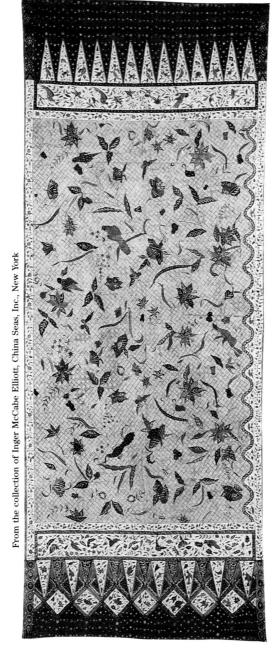

Woman's waistcloth (sarong)
Indonesia
Mid-20th century
Cotton, batik dyed

From the collection of Victoria and Albert Museum, London (T30.1928)

Bed curtain
England
Mid-17th century
Embroidered wool on cotton and linen
49″ × 78″ (124.5 × 198cm)

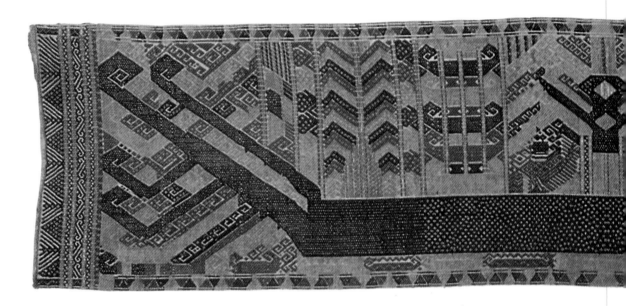

From the collection of The Textile Museum, Washington, D.C. (2984.45.4)

Palepai (**ship cloth**)
Sumatra (Indonesia)
8½ feet long (2.56m)

From the collection of Royal Ontario Museum, Toronto (919.6.11)

Robe (Imperial dragon)
China
c. 1750
Tapestry woven silk and gold

A work from the "World Tapestry Today" touring exhibition created by the American Tapestry Alliance

Tapestry
By Elène Gamache
Sillery, Quebec, Canada
1986

Decorative panel
Mexico
c. 1970
Embroidered cotton

Quilt (Hawaiian)
Designed by Deborah Kakalia, Honolulu
Made by Marjorie Kerr, Arvada, Colorado

Quilt
By Jean Hewes
Fort Worth, Texas
1981

Part Two

*Here are recommended ways to mount and frame
a textile—from casually draping it over a screen
to encapsulating it in a frame behind glass.*

*All of these recommendations safely preserve the
integrity of the textile without cutting, gluing,
stapling or nailing.*

Framing
and Mounting
Textile Art

Questions to Ask Before Selecting a Method of Framing and Mounting

- *What is the purpose of mounting and displaying this artwork?*
- *How should this artwork relate to the other furnishings?*
- *Can the textile be hung uncovered?*
- *Does the piece require visually strong framing?*
- *Will the present color of the wall give the desired contrast?*

Shawl from Cora Ginsburg Inc., New York.

English jacquard loom woven paisley shawl, c. 1860.

1 · Hung Freely

The hanging method of first choice is to allow the textile to hang freely, fully exposed. This permits a textile to reveal its unique quality: a soft tactile material, handmade and natural – its imperfections and draping adding a humanizing friendliness to a room.

Even a fragile textile made of thin material can be hung freely if it is sewn onto a sturdy cotton backing.

1A · Draped Over a Rod, Railing, Door or Screen

Rods

Brass tubing, wood dowel, or wood strip.

Wood should be covered with fabric or sealed with polyurethane varnish.

Advantages

- Easiest method of hanging.
- Permits periodic reversal of exposed side.
- Encourages creative non-symmetrical positioning of design.

Non-Symmetrical Positioning

Navajo blanket (Saltillo serape).

Navajo rug with symmetrical design precisely
in the middle.

Other less static positioning possibilities. This
method of hanging is also a good way to hide holes
or spots on textile.

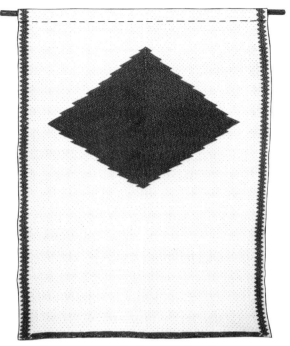

Hanging over a rod – top stitched back.

Hanging over a railing.

Hanging from a wood strip – bottom stitched back,
dowel inserted, ends protruding.

1B · Hanging from a Rod Pocket (Hanging Sleeve)

Rod pocket made by hand-sewing a heavy cotton sleeve across top of textile.

Advantages

- This is the traditional method of mounting textiles as wall tapestries.
- Permits even support for textiles which cannot be draped over a rod.
- Very easy to remove the textile for changing, inspecting or vacuuming.

Materials and Methods

Pocket material: washed, unbleached and undyed muslin, cotton, or canvas.

Sewing: Use single or double strand of cotton thread in a running backstitch. Insert the needle between warp threads.

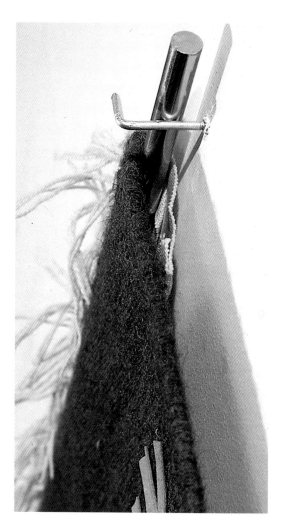

Mounting Through Holes Cut in Rod Pocket

Even a medium weight textile will make an end-supported rod sag in the middle. One solution: use a wood board as the hanging bar; attach hanging devices which protrude through holes in the rod pocket.

Measure and mark board into thirds. Attach picture mounts ⅓ of the way from each end.

After wood inserted into pocket, holes are cut for the rings of the picture mounts to protrude through the top of the rod pocket.

Photos show picture mounts connected to hanging wire, but the picture mounts can be hung directly onto "L" hooks in the wall.

Kilim-weave rug, Turkey; from Trocadero Textile Art, Washington.

Picture mounts attached to varnished wood board
1″ × 4″ (2.5 × 10 cm).

Hanging from Wire or Line

Materials

- Picture wire for heavy pieces.
- Fishing line (transparent).
- Mason line (non-stretching white string).

Advantage

By supporting the textile from the ceiling moulding or from hooks high up on the wall, the hanging height can be corrected or changed – without making new holes in the wall.

Method

- Pre-measure and cut the wire or line <u>before</u> attaching it to the rod.
- On plaster walls, screw hooks into plastic anchors (rawl plugs).

Hanging from "L" Hooks

Materials

- Mirror hanging plates.
- "L" hooks.

Advantages

- Hanging wire or line does not show.
- For large frames, or for frames hung high, the hooks are not visible – especially if they are later painted the color of the wall.

Back of frame, plates mounted.

Front of frame, hanging on "L" hooks.

Contemporary weaving, Mexico; from The Phoenix, Washington, D.C.

1C · Attaching with Velcro

The method of first choice for textiles which must be removed and remounted often. Because Velcro can hold 10 to 15 pounds per square inch (.710-1.065kg/sq cm), very heavy rugs and tapestries can be supported.

Advantages

• The top edge remains flat.
• The textile is very easy to remove for inspection and vacuuming.

How to Attach

1. Using 2″ wide (5 cm) Velcro, machine sew the looped side to 3″ wide (7.5 cm) cotton strip.

2. Using cotton thread, hand sew the top, bottom and sides of the strip to the textile. (If textile has been backed, stitch through both the backing and the textile.)

3. Staple the hooked side of the Velcro to a strip of varnished wood approximately 1″ × 4″ (2.5x10 cm).

4. Add hanging hardware to the strip of wood: screw eyes to the top edge, or hanging plates to the back side. Distance from end of strip: one-third width of textile.

5. Mark the center of the textile and the center of the board. Press the looped Velcro of the textile to the hooked Velcro of the board. Start at the center, then move outward.

6. (a) Mount pre-measured hanging wire to the wall. Lifting the board and the textile up together, attach wire to screw eyes on the wood strip.

   (b) Mount "L" hooks to the wall. Lifting the board and the textile up together, insert the "L" hooks into the hanging plates on the wood strip.

   (c) For permanent installations, the board may be bolted directly to the wall.

1D · Hanging with Rod Through Garment Sleeves

Appropriate for garments where shoulder line is straight across, such as for oriental robes.

Rod: bamboo, or wood dowel which has been varnished, lacquered or covered with cotton.

Man's robe, India.

Discouraging Theft of Framed Art

All metal frame manufacturers have safety locks available. Locks are also available for wood frames.

The UN Plaza Hotel in New York City has three or four framed textiles in each of its several hundred rooms. In ten years, only one textile has been stolen! Here is how they are mounted:

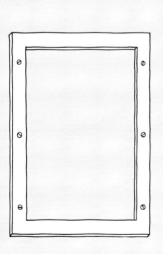

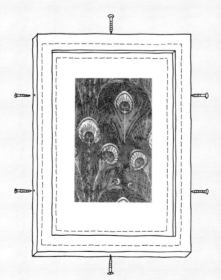

Rough wood frame screwed to wall.

Glass, mat, mounted textile and back board are laid into finished outer frame.

Outer frame positioned around rough mounting frame and screwed to it through the sides.

"Peacock Feather" printed fabric, designed by Arthur Silver, Liberty of London, 1887.

2 · Sewn to Backing Fabric Stretched Around Frame or Board

Advantages

- Gives better overall support to textile than hanging freely.
- Protects back from moths.
- Permits framing.

Materials

Strainers or stretchers: "clear" (no knots) sugar pine or poplar.

Board: Foam-core ¼″ or ⅜″ thick (6mm or 10mm).

Stretched fabric: Washed unbleached undyed cotton — lightweight muslin, normal weight cotton, or heavy weight canvas — depending upon the weight and size of the textile that it must support.

Method

- For small wood stretchers: mount stretched fabric to frame with staples.
  Pin textile onto stretched fabric.
  Hand-sew textile to stretched fabric.

- For large stretchers or foam-core board: mount stretched fabric temporarily.
  Pin textile onto stretched fabric.
  Mark location of stretcher corners on the stretched fabric.
  Remove stretched fabric.
  Sew textile to fabric.
  Re-mount stretched fabric. (Use staples on wood. Use carpet tape or white glue on back side of board.)

Sewing

- Use silk thread on silk; on all else, use cotton.
  For very heavy textiles, use double strand of thread.
  Sew with running backstitch, i.e., loops.

- For lightweight textiles which could sag, tack at other places on the textile — preferably on seams or at design lines.

2A · Hanging without Frame or Covering

If the mounted textile has its own border, use a backing material with a color which blends with the wall color. If the mounted textile does not have a strong border design, select a backing material which contrasts with the wall color.

When the stretched backing is mounted without a frame, the staples must be on the back, not on the sides of the stretcher.

Uzbek ikat, from Douglas Dawson Gallery, Chicago.

See cover photo of this mounted textile hung on a white wall.

2B · Adding a Plastic Cover

Advantages

- Gives full view of textile without visual detractions.
- Protects textile from dust and touching.
- Could be made of ultraviolet-blocking plastic: Plexiglas UF3, Lucite AR or Perspex VA.

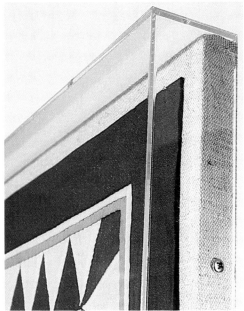

Hmong appliqué.

Acrylic ("Plexiglas," Lucite," "Perspex") shadow box screwed to edges of stretcher. Use Phillips-head screws in countersunk holes.

Indian embroidery.

2C · Framing Around Stretcher

Frame may be wood or metal.

Stretcher in metal frame (Neilson #71). Clip springs hold the stretcher tightly in frame.

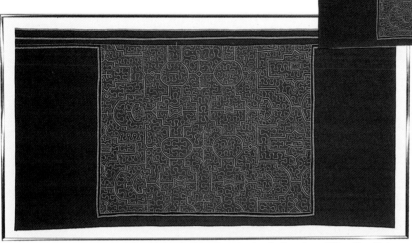

Embroidered skirt, made by Shipibo Indians, Peruvian jungle; from Luna D'Oro, New York.

Wood strips may be nailed to stretcher. Corners need not be mitered.

Wood: "1 × 2 clear maple slat" (which is actually ¾″ × 1½″).

Stain: Walnut – or other colors.

Nails: Wire brads with small heads.

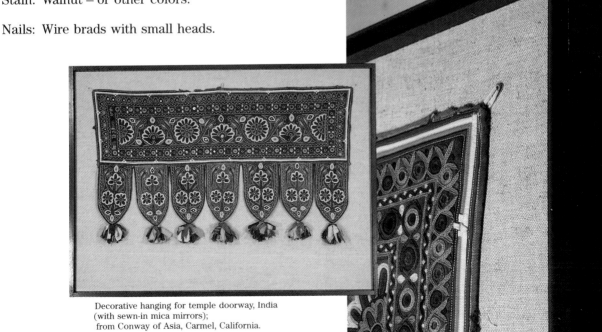

Decorative hanging for temple doorway, India
(with sewn-in mica mirrors);
from Conway of Asia, Carmel, California.

3 · Framed Behind Glass or Plastic

Recommended for small fragile textiles and fragments.

Advantages

- Provides protection from humidity, dust, insects and touching.
- Displays textile with an elegance and drama which says, "This is an important piece."
- Protects against ultraviolet light (UV) if covered with UV blocking plastic (Plexiglas UF3, Lucite AR or Perspex VA).
- Gives opportunity to use mat color which contrasts with the color of the wall.
- Frame can be on the floor leaning against the wall, on a shelf or on an easel.

Hanging

If frame is hung from back wire, always hang it from two nails or hooks — widely spaced — regardless of how light the piece may be.

3A · Framing Under Mat

Thin textile fragments may be pinned to board and placed under a mat.

Pins should be thin and non-rusting (insect mounting pins) and inserted between the threads of the textile.

Mounting board and mat should be acid-free ("museum board").

For added elegance, mat may be wrapped with silk or linen.

Indian sari fragment.

3B · Floating in Multiple Mat Separator

Especially appropriate for thicker textiles which
have a border design.

Advantage: Textile not covered or touched by mat.

Method

Textile sewn to backing fabric, which is then
wrapped around acid-free board.

Textile separated from glass by two or three
thicknesses of mat board.

Indonesian ship cloth, from Mia Gallery, Seattle.

3C · A Metal Frame with Separation Channels

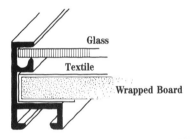

Frame channel profile typical of Nielsen #55,
Designer #50, Designer #52 and Clark #600.

These channels are available in many metallic
finishes and black. They are easily assembled
with a screwdriver.

Belgian lace handkerchiefs.

3D · Framing with Spacers or Set-Backs

Advantages

- Increases the choice of frame styles that can be used.
- Textile separated away from glass or plastic.

Spacers/set-backs

- Wood (same wood as frame).
- Plastic strips wrapped in same cloth that the textile is mounted on.
- Transparent plastic channel (which fits around edge of glass).
- Plastic spacers (for use with plastic).

Persian brocade, from Trocadero Textile Art, Washington.

In the example above, note that the spacer and the frame color are selected to have the least possible visual interference with the textile — which has its own strong border.

3E · Pressure Mounting

In low humidity conditions, a textile may be temporarily mounted without a mat or spacer — the plastic pressing directly against the textile. This method is especially useful for mounting delicate fragments.

Mola, Cuna Indians, San Blas Islands, Panama; from Luna D'Oro, New York.

Use plastic. Do not use glass, which has a high acid content. The mounting should use some "blotting" material inside the frame — such as washed unbleached muslin or rag board — to absorb any moisture.

To prevent the textile from slipping down inside the frame, lay a piece of cotton flannel or acid-free foam plastic sheeting under the textile.

Pressure mounting is not recommended for permanent framing.

4 · Enclosed in Clear Plastic Box

Advantage

Textile given full view, with full protection.

Box material: Acrylic plastic panel.

Top of box can be snap-on lid so that textile can be removed.

Rod and bracket are plastic.

Mounting and Framing Options

Unmounted Bolivian dress panel.

Same textile partially turned back over a foam board which is covered with white canvas.

The textile is held in place by the black frame and hangs freely, uncovered by glass or plastic. The turned back portion has not been cut away – it is still there on the back of the frame.

The framing gives the textile greater size and a more commanding presence, especially when hung on a wood, travertine or tan wall.

Same textile partially turned back over a wooden dowel rod.

The turn-back gives the piece a strong horizontal shape, instead of the uninteresting square shape. The thick wood dowel gives the piece added visual strength.

Because less than half is turned back, the turn-back is lightly sewn to prevent it from slipping off the rod.

Same textile sewn (top only) to tan linen, which is wrapped around foam board. The piece hangs freely and is uncovered. Frame is walnut. The top of the board has an arch of russet ultrasuede, picking up one of the colors of the stripes.

The framing is designed for a white wall.

Low-Impact Textile Becomes High-Impact Wall Decor via Dramatic Framing

A textile without strong design and without strong border can be dramatized by high-contrast mounting, imbalanced positioning, and high-contrast framing.

In this example, the framing also visually enlarges the size of the textile.

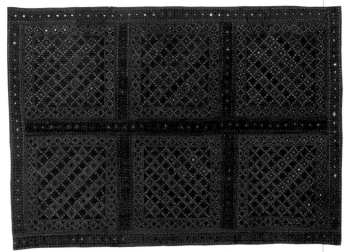

Indian embroidery (with sewn-in glass mirrors); from Gallery of Stray Thoughts, Wilmette, Illinois.

Light-Colored Mat Floats
Dark Textile on Dark Wall

Dark textile sewn to canvas that is then wrapped around foam board. Frame is gold-colored metal.

To add intimacy, the textile is left uncovered, without glass or plastic.

Child's crib quilt, Amish.

Part Three

Carefully positioned art can be a center of focus, can establish unity, create sanctuary and set the mood of the space.

Thoughtful positioning creates the first good impression — making people feel welcome.

Positioning Art

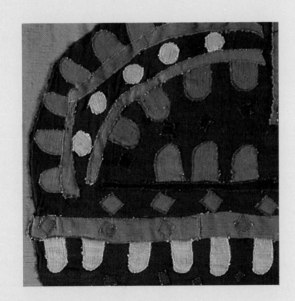

Basics of Positioning

1. Select small size, small pattern art for small rooms.

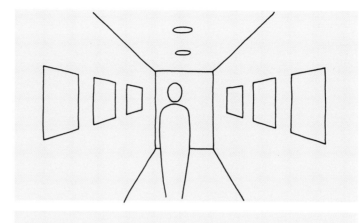

2. Select large size, large pattern art for large rooms.

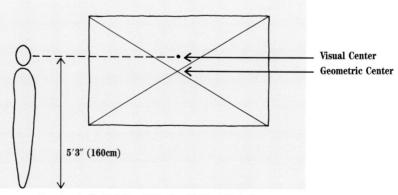

3. Use small art near the entrance to a space; use large art at the far end of the space.

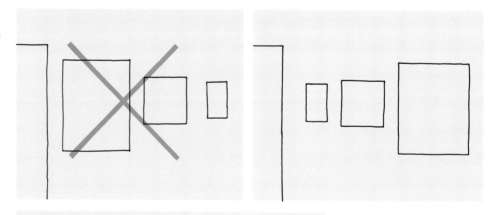

4. Position art so its visual center is at eye height: 5′3″ (160cm).

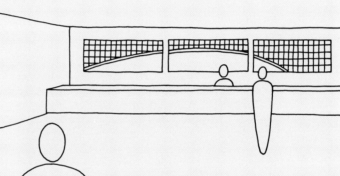

Drawings by Yoshi Sekiguchi Design, Highland Park, IL.

5. Position art low in a space where people sit down: restaurants, waiting rooms, conference rooms.

6. Place a comparatively small artwork off-center and low on a large wall.

7. Match the scale of the art to the surrounding furnishings.

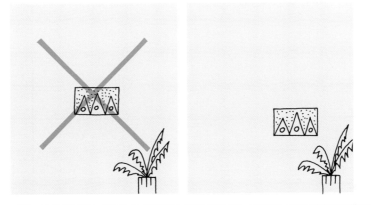

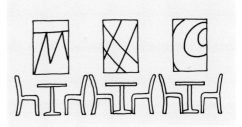

8. Intermix art with other decorative furnishings so that the grouping is relaxed and informal, avoiding rigid geometric balance.

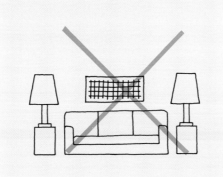

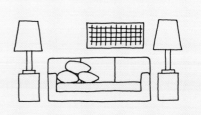

Art Plus Plants

Textile art and plants are frequent allies. Plants can:

- *Create a visual bridge to the art.*
- *Form an inoffensive barrier against people touching the art.*
- *Hide lights shining on the art.*
- *Reinforce greens and blues in the art.*

Plants do not need special lights. The same type and color lights which illuminate the art can also provide growing light to the plants.

To prevent plants from transmitting insects to the textile, the plants should be sprayed before bringing them into the same room as the textile (especially if the textile is unframed).

When positioned, the plants should not touch the textile or the frame. The textile should be protected from being splashed when the plants are watered.

Except for these obvious precautions, plants and textiles are compatible companions.

Where Textile Art Should <u>Not</u> Be Placed

- In direct or reflected sunlight.
- Over heat vents or radiators.
- Under hot bright lights.
- Over hot wires.
- Near flames or candles.
- Where food or water can splash on it.
- Touching the floor – or even near the floor.
- Against a cold outside wall where moisture can condense.
- Where it is inconvenient to reach or remove for cleaning.

Surprise Placement

Textile art lends itself to placements and positions beyond the "square against the wall" of paintings, prints or posters. Textiles can have surprise placement creating informality, demonstrating imagination – even showing light-hearted whimsy. Some of the possibilities:

- Draped over a door, screen or railing.
- Draped to form a canopy.
- Stretched across the ceiling.
- Placed on an easel, on a shelf, or on the floor, or leaning against a wall.

Ship cloth (Sumatra, Indonesia). Page 67 shows framing.

Framed artwork on easel hides ugly radiator.

Saying "Welcome"

A banner, quilt or tapestry at the entrance of a hotel, office building or restaurant visually proclaims, "We're glad you came. We hope you like being here."

The textile art should be colorful, free-flowing and large, but not overpowering. The center of focus should be low. The design should be simple. Curves are more welcoming than rigid geometrics and precise grids.

Before: Five thousand people a day enter this lobby and walk down the stairway (under horizontal walkway) en route to their suburban trains.

Banners: appliqued nylon 13' × 10' (3.96 × 3m)

After: Red banners call out "Here is where the bank is. Look how close it is. You are welcome to come up."

Pointing Direction

Designers should imagine how a traveler would feel: weary from a long flight, arms weighted with bags, entering a cathedral-sized lobby, not knowing which direction to turn.... Textile art can lead the eye to the reception desk.

The photograph below shows how textile art can help visitors find the reception desk hidden in the far corner of a large high lobby in an office building.

Wall hanging helps visitors find the reception desk in this large, high-ceiling lobby.

Textile art can also point direction by using a series of banners which leads the eye from entrance to reception, or to the elevators. Such a series should have a communality of shape, design and color.

Creating a Center of Focus

Very large spaces — shopping malls, hotels with atriums, airports, department stores, etc. — should have one easily seen, unique, point-of-focus to give people a sense of direction and a place to meet.

Used as a center of focus, textile art can be multiple sections hung together to form a three-dimensional shape. Another way of mounting: sections of textiles mounted on a metal framework.

In these uses, the textiles should be above reach and should not have any horizontally draped elements that could hold water from a leaking roof or hold refuse thrown down from upper floors.

Creating Sanctuary

Sanctuary, a feeling of being separated and safe, is like sitting on a bench under a tree on a sunny day as the traffic hurries by.

For a bar or restaurant area within a high ceiling space, sanctuary can be created with a series of low hanging banners over the area. The banners should have visual unity by being the same color or the same design in different colors. The textiles can be draped to form a canopy if there are no open floors above it (and if approved by fire code).

Tapestry by Henry Easterwood, Memphis, Tennessee. Art Consultant: Jean Efron, Washington

Large tapestry defines a space which is off to the side of a large, high-ceiling office building lobby.

Red and set low, the tapestry's hearthlike warmth invites people to come over and sit down.

The photo above shows another way that textile art can create sanctuary: A very large tapestry — with warm colors, non-geometric design and low detailing — establishes a place, a scale and a mood.

Creating Unity

Sometimes a space is broken up by an elevator bank, a fire door or an "L" turn. Textile art can create unity and continuity by using a series of pieces: the same design in different colors, or a series of designs in the same color. However, the more variation between pieces of the series, the less effective the unity. There is nothing wrong with having all the pieces of the series exactly the same.

The photograph below shows another way of creating unity with textile art: visually enclosing an area with one very long piece, or with a series of similar pieces. To achieve this unit, the pieces must be visually similar in color and design.

Tapestry by Akiko Kotani, Slippery Rock, Pennsylvania

Panoramic triptych tapestry, with strong design, ties together tables and chairs to define a space. The earth colors and non-geometric design help soften the sterile geometric alignment of lights, wall tile and carpet pattern.

Also See

Part 2 Framing and Mounting: suggestions on selecting frames, mats and backgrounds to contrast with wall color.

Part 5 Care and Maintenance: suggestions on correcting problems of heat and light.

Entire Hotel Decorated with Textile Art

The only art on the walls of the United Nations Plaza Hotel in New York City is textile art — historic and ethnographic.

Framed textile art hangs in the lobby, each dining room, all meeting rooms, the hallways on every floor and in each guest room — sometimes two or three in each room!

The textile art softens the crisply modern design of the hotel created by Kevin Roche John Dinkeloo and Associates, of Hamden, Connecticut. Mae Festa of Roche-Dinkeloo selected the textiles, planned the framing and supervised the positioning.

The textiles that she selected range from rare Chinese embroidery to imaginatively-framed fragments of old dresses found in flea markets.

Courtesy of the United Nations Development Corp.

Tampan from Sumatra (Indonesia) in a guest room.

Courtesy of the United Nations Development Corp.

Section of brocaded sash from Indonesia.

Part Four

Selecting the appropriate lighting for artwork is part of the creative realization.

After giving so much care selecting or creating an artwork, it would be unfortunate if it can not be seen because it does not have enough light, if it is destroyed by lights that are too bright, or if it turns ugly because the lights are the wrong color.

Lighting Art

Courtesy of Tech Lighting, Chicago

Planning the Lighting

1. What is the designer's goal:

   To create a visual focal point?

   To attract the eye to a specific location?

   To lower the scale of the walls?

   To add textural enrichment?

   To add color accent?

   To repeat a color or pattern in other decorative accessories?

2. Is special lighting required beyond normal natural daylight and the planned artificial lighting of the space?

3. Does the shape, size or texture of the textile require special consideration?

4. Where can light fixtures (luminaires) be mounted? How far away is the light source from the textile? What are the restrictions on the angle of lighting?

5. Which bulbs/lamps could be used? Would hot-spots be eliminated if more than one bulb/lamp is used?

6. Does the fiber of the textile require special protection from ultraviolet rays, brightness or heat?

7. Should the wiring include timers and dimmers?

How Much Light Can Shine on Textile Art?

The light selection charts on pages 88, 89, 90 and 91 tell exactly which light bulbs or tubes to install. All you need to know is the size of the artwork and the distance of the light fixture from the wall.

These charts are based on shining 30 foot-candles of light on the art eight hours a day, six days a week. This level of illumination is acceptable for contemporary textile art, typically commercially dyed wool, cotton or synthetic blends. (Illumination can be measured with a light meter. Many light meters used in photography have a "Foot-Candle" scale.)

- A foot-candle of light is the amount of light striking a one-foot square area one foot from a candle.

- A lux of light is approximately equal to 10 foot-candles.

Early textiles or delicate textiles can safely be exposed to 15 foot-candles of light.

Museum-quality textiles – delicate, fragile and irreplaceable – can safely be exposed to 3 - 5 foot-candles of light if periodically rotated. This is one-tenth the light level in a typical 50 foot-candle office!

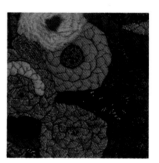

Positioning the Distance of the Light

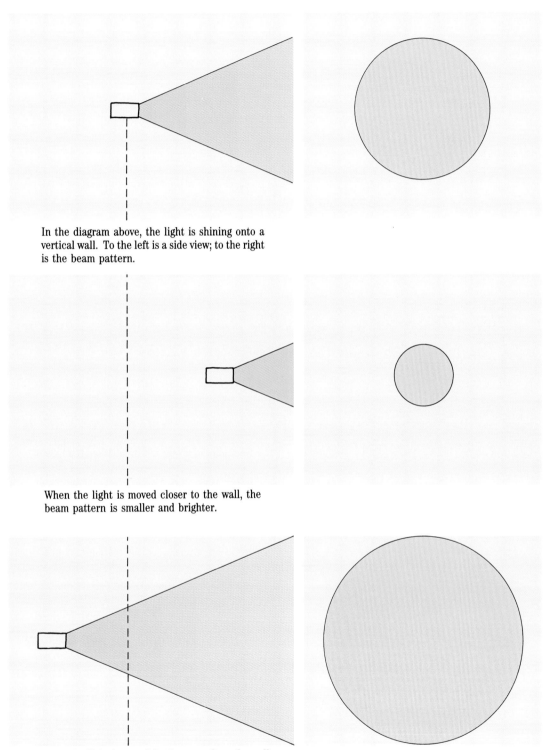

In the diagram above, the light is shining onto a vertical wall. To the left is a side view; to the right is the beam pattern.

When the light is moved closer to the wall, the beam pattern is smaller and brighter.

When the light is moved further away from the wall, the beam pattern is larger, but the light is not as bright.

Positioning the Angle of Light

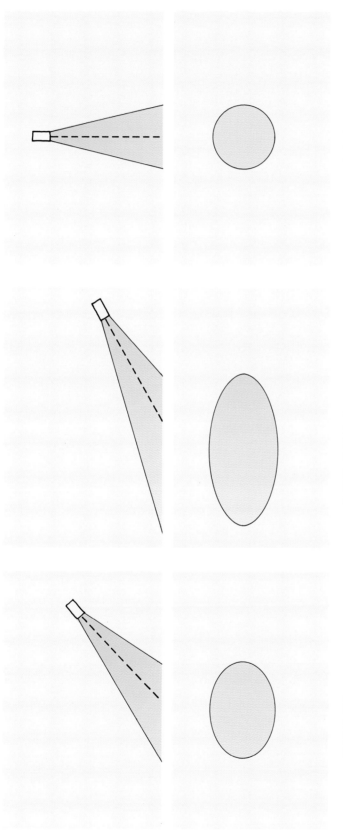

When the light shines directly onto the wall, the beam pattern is not distorted. But there is an unpleasant glare reflected off the wall and the art.

When the light shines downward, the beam pattern becomes oval shaped. In addition, the light is brighter at the top of the oval than at the bottom of the oval.

Light pointed too steeply downward accents imperfections, over-accents the texture, or puts deep shadows onto three-dimensional sculpturing.

A practical compromise is to set the light so that it points 45 degrees downward.

The lamp selection charts on pages 88 to 91 are based on the light shining downward at a 45-degree angle to the artwork.

Measuring the Distance and Angle

1. Position the artwork.

2. Measure the distance from the visual center of the artwork to the height of the light (distance **A**).

3. Place the light this same distance away from the wall that the artwork is on (distance **B**).

When vertical distance **A** (visual center of art to height of light) is the same as the horizontal distance **B** (light to wall), the light will be at a 45 degree angle when pointed at the visual center of the artwork.

The distance **C**, from the light to the visual center of the art, is the "throw-distance."

When the light is pointed at a 45-degree angle downward, the throw-distance is 1.4 longer than the distance the light is from the wall ($C = 1.4B$).

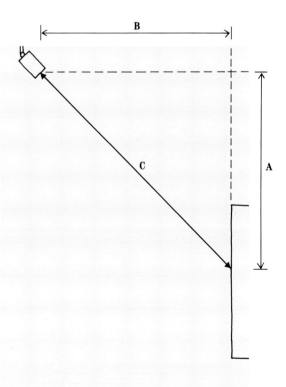

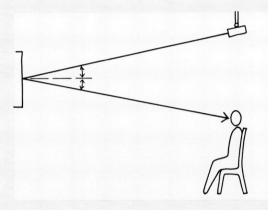

Overcoming Glare

Artwork that is covered with glass or plastic can reflect light into the eyes of people nearby. The potential for glare can be determined even before the artwork is hung because the angle of light reflection is always the same as the angle of the light on the art.

Here are four solutions to the problem of glare:

- *Add parabolic louvers to fixture, which provide a 45 degree shielding angle.*

- *Set the ceiling lights at a sharper angle: move the lights closer to the wall where the art is displayed.*

- *Use floor canisters that shine light upward.*

- *Remove the glass or plastic!*

Do not use non-reflecting glass on textiles: Non-reflecting glass only works if it is pressed directly against the artwork. Glass of any kind is acidic; it should not press against valuable textiles.

Dramatizing Colors

Incandescent Light

Swatch board lighted with a bulb that is high on the red end of the color spectrum.

Warm colors—red, orange and brown—are enhanced by lamps with warm colored light: incandescent bulbs, such as standard household lights, incandescent PAR-38s, and continuous glass-envelope lamps: A's, P's ER's and R's.

Dimming any of these makes them redder.

Danger Blue swatch #3 looks almost black; lighter blue swatches #4, #5, #6, #7 and #9 are grayed; brown #11 becomes russet; russet #14 becomes orangy.

Halogen Light

The same swatch board lighted with a halogen light.

A more balanced light is emitted by halogen lamps and bulbs: low voltage MR-16, and PAR-36; standard household voltage PAR-20, PAR-30, PAR-38, T-3 and T-4 tubes.

"Halogen," "tungsten-halogen" and "quartz-halogen" are the same light-wise. It is only necessary to say "halogen."

Halogen light is visually less blue than daylight and less red than incandescent. Yet, to eyes accustomed to seeing objects under warm incandescent light, halogen has a crisp, almost icy, whiteness.

Sunlight

The same swatch board in light that is high on the blue end of the color spectrum.

Cool colors—blue and green—are enhanced by daylight.

Danger Gray #2 becomes light blue; yellow #8 is given a green cast; all browns and reds are darkened, with dark brown #12 almost turning black.

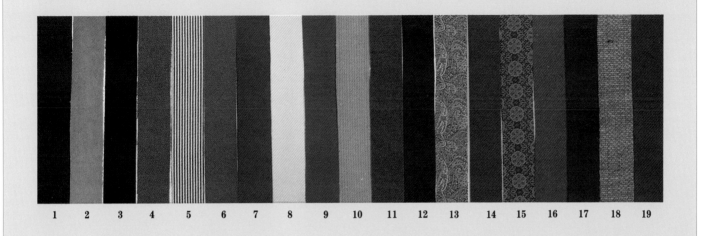

1 2 3 4 5 6 7 8 9 10 11 12 13 14 15 16 17 18 19

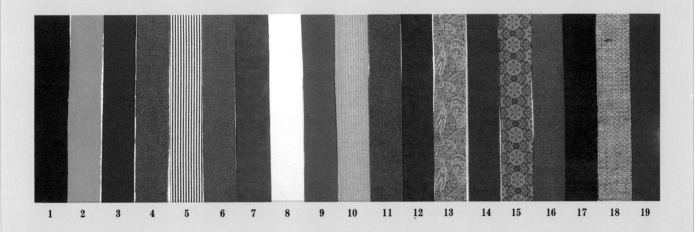

1 2 3 4 5 6 7 8 9 10 11 12 13 14 15 16 17 18 19

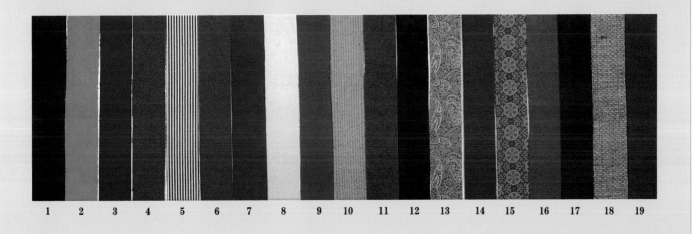

1 2 3 4 5 6 7 8 9 10 11 12 13 14 15 16 17 18 19

Selecting the Appropriate Light

This chart describes lights that cover a 3 foot (.91m) circle with light at least 30 foot-candles bright. The lights are in three groups:

- Low voltage halogen
- Standard voltage halogen
- Standard voltage incandescent

How to Use This Chart

1. Decide if the lights should be incandescent or halogen, low-voltage halogen or line-voltage halogen. (The chart lists the pros and cons.)

2. Look down the column showing the height and width of the beam pattern. Put a check beside those lamps that have a beam pattern larger than the artwork.

3. Look down the light-to-wall column. Put a check beside those lamps that have a distance close to the present position of the lights.

   Or, look down the art-to-light column and put a check beside those lamps that have a distance suited to positioning the art so that the visual center of the art is at eye level.

   To set lights at a 45 degree angle downward, the distance from the visual center of the art to the height of the light must be the same as the distance from the light to the wall.

4. If more than one lamp meets the dimensional requirements of both positioning and beam size, then use the lamp with the lowest wattage.

Fine Tuning

Throw-distance, light coverage area and brightness are interrelated in this way:

- The closer the light, the brighter and smaller the area of light coverage; the farther the light, the dimmer and larger the coverage.

- The closer a ceiling mounted light is to the wall, the greater the distortion of the beam pattern in both shape and brightness.

- Shining the light at a steeper angle lowers the brightness on the art. A flatter angle increases the brightness.

- Small changes in distance cause significant changes in brightness. For example, a light that is moved from 10 feet away to 5 feet away is not twice as bright, but <u>four times</u> as bright. (Inversely proportional to the square of the distance.)

For further fine-tuning, there is a wide choice of devices and lenses that attach to the light fixture to change the beam pattern size, shape and brightness.

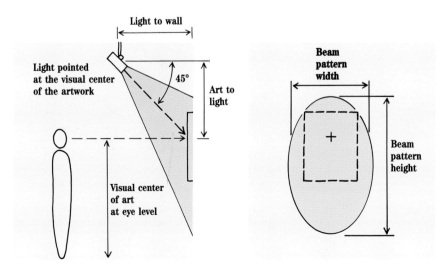

Low-Voltage Halogen

Description

Designed to operate at 12 volts (can also be set for 6 volts or 5 volts). Because standard line voltage is higher (120V or 220V), the voltage must be stepped down.

One way to do this: Use one transformer on the entire track of fixtures. (Simple solution, but erratic operation.) Another way: Use fixtures that have individual transformers built into each one of them. (More expensive, but reliable.)

Pros

- Tight, precisely focused beam of crisp white light.
- Power efficient.
- Many fixture accessories available.
- MR-16 (dichroic low voltage halogen reflector lamp) reflects most of its heat backwards.
- MR-16, only 2″ in diameter, is very inconspicuous.

Cons

- Bulbs burn very hot.
- 75W MR-16 burns especially hot and has a short life.

Halogen low-voltage lamps that can throw 30 foot-candles of light on a circle 3 feet (.91m) in diameter or larger.*

Light to wall

Art to light

Must be same for 45° angle.

		Candle-power	Beam Spread	Light to wall Ft.	M	Art to light Ft.	M	Beam pattern height Ft.	M	Beam pattern width Ft.	M
	50W MR-16 FL	1,500	40°	4′3″	1.28 m	4′3″	1.28 m	6′1″	1.85 m	4′4″	1.31 m
	65W MR-16 FL	2,000	38°	4′10″	1.48 m	4′10″	1.48 m	6′6″	1.97 m	4′7″	1.40 m
	36W PAR-36 WFL	2,350	30°	5′3″	1.59 m	5′3″	1.59 m	5′7″	1.70 m	3′11″	1.19 m
	50W MR-16 NFL	3,000	26°	6′0″	1.82 m	6′0″	1.82 m	5′5″	1.65 m	3′10″	1.17 m
	65W MR-16 NFL	4,000	23°	6′10″	2.09 m	6′10″	2.09 m	5′6″	1.67 m	3′11″	1.19 m
	50W MR-16 NSP	9,150	13°	10′5″	3.17 m	10′5″	3.17 m	4′7″	1.41 m	3′3″	0.99 m
	65W MR-16 NSP	11,500	14°	11′8″	3.55 m	11′8″	3.55 m	5′8″	1.72 m	4′0″	1.22 m

*Despite the same name and code number, lamps from different manufacturers have slightly different beam spread angles. That is why after each lamp listed above, the candle-power and beam spread are shown.

If a lamp (with the same name and code number) has a narrower beam spread, it will illuminate a smaller area and it will probably be slightly brighter than 30 foot-candles. "Fine Tuning" tells how to adjust for this.

What the Lamp-Code Designations Mean

ER   Specially focused R reflector lamp.

FL   Flood. Has wide beam spread and usually has textured lens.

MR   Miniature reflector.

NFL   Narrow flood.

NSP   Narrow spot.

PAR   Parabolic aluminized reflector.

SP   Spot. Has tight beam focus and usually has clear lens.

R   Reflector.

T   Tubular lamp.

W   Watts (power rating).

WFL   Wide flood.

Cool

Lamps that do not throw all their heat onto the object being lit.

(The removed heat is either absorbed by special sockets and special fixtures, or the heat is reflected backward by a special coating on the lens and dispersed out the back of an open fixture.)

Size

A number not followed by a W (watts) designates the physical diameter of the glass envelope, in eighths-of-an-inch.

(Size has nothing to do with brightness!)

Example

"75W PAR-38 FL" is read as "seventy-five-watt par-thirty-eight flood." This lamp is 4¾″ in diameter (38/8).

Line-Voltage Halogen

Description

The best of both worlds: a halogen bulb that can be screwed into a standard line voltage socket—without requiring a transformer.

Pros

• Tight, precisely focused beam of crisp white light. (Noticeably whiter than incandescent lamps.)

• Lower operating cost than incandescent. (A 90W halogen is as bright as a 150W incandescent!)

Cons

• Higher initial purchase price than incandescent.
• Bulbs get very hot.
• Leaving them on dim continuously shortens their life.
• Some brands have a noticeable flicker.

Line-voltage halogen lamps that can throw 30 foot-candles of light on a circle 3 feet (.91m) in diameter or larger.*

Must be same for 45° angle.

		Candle-power	Beam Spread	Light to wall		Art to light		Beam pattern height		Beam pattern width	
				Ft.	M	Ft.	M	Ft.	M	Ft.	M
	50W PAR-20 NFL	1,250	32°	3'10"	1.17 m	3'10"	1.17 m	4'4"	1.32 m	3'1"	0.94 m
	75W PAR-30 FL	1,800	42°	4'7"	1.40 m	4'7"	1.40 m	6'11"	2.10 m	4'11"	1.49 m
	75W PAR-30 NFL	3,000	32°	5'11"	1.80 m	5'11"	1.80 m	6'8"	2.04 m	4'9"	1.44 m
	90W PAR-38 FL	4,000	30°	6'10"	2.09 m	6'10"	2.09 m	7'3"	2.20 m	5'1"	1.56 m
	150W PAR-38 FL	7,500	30°	9'5"	2.87 m	9'5"	2.87 m	9'8"	2.96 m	6'11"	2.10 m
	90W PAR-38 SP (Cool)	10,000	15°	10'11"	3.32 m	10'11"	3.32 m	5'6"	1.68 m	3'11"	1.19 m
	90W PAR-38 NSP	22,500	9°	16'4"	4.97 m	16'4"	4.97 m	4'11"	1.49 m	3'6"	1.07 m
	150W PAR-38 SP	25,000	10°	17'2"	5.24 m	17'2"	5.24 m	5'9"	1.76 m	4'1"	1.25 m
	150W PAR-38 NSP	37,500	9°	21'0"	6.41 m	21'0"	6.41 m	6'2"	1.89 m	4'5"	1.34 m

*Despite the same name and code number, lamps from different manufacturers have slightly different beam spread angles. That is why after each lamp listed above, the candle-power and beam spread are shown.

If a lamp (with the same name and code number) has a narrower beam spread, it will illuminate a smaller area and it will probably be slightly brighter than 30 foot-candles. "Fine Tuning" tells how to adjust for this.

Halogen Tubular Lamp in Wide-Flood Fixture ("Wall-Washer")

Standard line-voltage halogen lamps are also available as raw light sources (such as "T-3" and "T-4"). A fixture is required to focus and shape the light beam. The advantage of this lamp/fixture combination is that it can provide a wide beam of bright light to cover a large horizontal area. A lens may be attached to the fixture to flatten the light and to reduce hot spots at the top of the rectangular beam pattern.

There is a choice of many halogen tubular lamp wattages (100W to 500W) and many fixture designs. Here are two typical lamp/ fixture combinations showing the wide beam pattern that can be achieved at a short distance. Both provide 30 foot-candles of illumination. Both are pointed downward 45 degrees.

	Tube Size	Beam Spread	Light to wall		Art to light		Beam pattern height		Beam pattern width	
			Ft.	M	Ft.	M	Ft.	M	Ft.	M
Lightolier "Preview Flood"	150W T-4	65° × 70°	3'0"	.91 m	3'0"	.91 m	5'11"	1.80 m	12'11"	3.93 m
Lightolier Adjustable "Power Flood"	250W T-4	65° × 80°	4'0"	1.22 m	4'0"	1.22 m	9'6"	2.90 m	17'2"	5.24 m

Incandescent

Description

Incandescent lights were the early original bulbs designed to screw into standard line-voltage sockets.

Later they were defined to encompass all non-fluorescent lamps.

The understood definition now: All glowing-filament bulbs except halogen.

Pros

• Low purchase price.
• Widely available at hardware stores and electric shops.
• Warm color is "friendly" and flattering to face color.
• Can be dimmed (making them even redder).
• Most manufacturers make cool-beam lamps that throw less heat forward onto the object being lighted.

Cons

High operating cost because they are very inefficient compared with fluorescent or halogen.

The very early continuous glass envelope bulbs, A's and R's, are so costly to operate that they should not even be used if the lights are on all day, every day.

Incandescent lamps that can throw 30 foot-candles of light on a circle 3 feet (.91m) in diameter or larger.*

Light to wall

Art to light

Must be same for 45° angle.

Beam pattern height

Beam pattern width

		Candle-power	Beam Spread	Ft.	M	Ft.	M	Ft.	M	Ft.	M
	100W R-40 FL	900	76°	3'3"	0.99 m	3'3"	0.99 m	10'0"	3.05 m	7'1"	2.16 m
	75W ER-30 FL	1,500	35°	4'3"	1.28 m	4'3"	1.28 m	5'0"	1.52 m	3'7"	1.09 m
	75W PAR-38 FL (Cool)	1,800	30°	4'7"	1.41 m	4'7"	1.41 m	4'10"	1.46 m	3'5"	1.04 m
	120W ER-40 FL	2,350	35°	5'3"	1.59 m	5'3"	1.59 m	6'4"	1.92 m	4'6"	1.37 m
	100W PAR-38 FL	2,400	30°	5'4"	1.62 m	5'4"	1.62 m	6'0"	1.82 m	4'0"	1.22 m
	150W PAR-38 FL (Cool)	4,000	30°	6'10"	2.09 m	6'10"	2.09 m	7'2"	2.19 m	5'1"	1.55 m
	75W PAR-38 SP	4,500	15°	7'3"	2.22 m	7'3"	2.22 m	3'9"	1.14 m	2'8"	0.81 m
	100W R-40 SP	5,000	22°	7'8"	2.34 m	7'8"	2.34 m	5'9"	1.76 m	4'1"	1.25 m
	100W PAR-38 SP	6,600	15°	8'10"	2.69 m	8'10"	2.69 m	4'6"	1.37 m	3'2"	0.98 m
	150W PAR-38 SP (Cool)	11,500	15°	11'8"	3.55 m	11'8"	3.55 m	6'0"	1.82 m	4'3"	1.29 m

*Despite the same name and code number, lamps from different manufacturers have slightly different beam spread angles. That is why after each lamp listed above, the candle-power and beam spread are shown.

If a lamp (with the same name and code number) has a narrower beam spread, it will illuminate a smaller area and it will probably be slightly brighter than 30 foot-candles. "Fine Tuning" tells how to adjust for this.

Lamps Not Recommended for Lighting Art

Fluorescent

• Can not throw focused beam of light.
• Many fluorescents have high ultraviolet ray emission (although the UV can be shielded with tube sleeves or UV blocking screen on fixture).

Metal Halide

• Have blue color and high UV emission (although both can be corrected with filters and UV screens).

Sodium Vapor

• Only emit a yellow colored light. (Can not be corrected.)

Testing Colors and Lights Before Ordering

Major lighting distributors have showrooms where architects, designers and artists can check materials under varying light. There is no charge for this service.

There are two ways to use this resource:

Artists can select colors after finding out what kind of lighting will be used in the planned space.

Artists can select lamps that are best for their artwork, then specify that similar lamps be used in the installation.

Adjusting Lights to Emphasize One Place or Area

The light beam pattern does not have to be centered on the artwork. Here are two alternate positionings.

Lights are not centered, but positioned to accent the design.

The <u>color</u> of the lights can also be selected to enhance the design—even if different colored lights are used on the same artwork.

Lights on large high artwork are set low to bring down the scale.

*Improper mounting is the major danger
in textile art.*

*Other dangers are sunlight,
excessive heat and insects.*

*Here is how to prevent or cure these dangers
and other less likely dangers.*

Care and Maintenance of Textiles

Introduction to Care and Maintenance

Where is the middle-ground between:

- *Treating textiles as if they were religious icons, touchable only by priests wearing white gloves.*

- *Destroying textiles by acts of criminal negligence: nailing them to the wall, taping them to corrugated cardboard, hanging them in direct sunlight, storing them tightly folded in a hot attic or damp basement?*

Millions of people have been making textiles for hundreds of years. There are hundreds of thousands of blouses, robes, rugs, saris, sashes, shawls and skirts. Only a tiny percent are of such rare quality that they should be locked away under controlled temperature and humidity.

How should the rest be evaluated? By what the collector paid for it? By how the maker valued it? The correct evaluation is based on the artistic merit of the object: form, proportion, balance, color, texture, material, workmanship. To these, add the intellectual appeal: how it was made, how it was used, what it means.

It doesn't matter if you bought it for a pack of cigarettes from a shepherd's wife. If it is a great piece, it has value. It should be treated with respect and cared for.

Taking care of textile art is quite simple. The following part, Care and Maintenance, tells the most likely dangers and how to avoid them or correct them.

Unfortunately, not all criminal destruction of artwork can be cured by providing information. There is still the "potlatch problem": people who deliberately treat artworks with cavalier disregard, as though the destruction gauges how well they can afford to discard objects of obvious value.

We should not be in such awe of wealth that we are afraid to speak up and say, "It is a crime to destroy objects of rare beauty!"

1 · Sunlight (Also see #2: Artificial Light.)

Danger

- Sunlight causes fading and the breakdown of textile fibers. Even sunlight reflected from a mirror is destructive. The damage is cumulative and irreversible!

- The danger is from three sources: the visible light, the ultraviolet (UV) rays, and the infra-red (heat) rays. Glass windows only partially block UV rays; damaging rays <u>do</u> come through.

- Fibers most vulnerable: jute, silk, wool, cotton, linen, nylon, acetate, rayon.

- All colors are vulnerable to fading, especially colors made from vegetable dyes and from synthetic dyes made before 1933. In general, dark colors, especially blues and black, are more likely to fade than light colors.

Prevention

- Do not permit sunlight or reflected sunlight to shine on textiles.

- Use fibers which have better resistance to sunlight: glass, acrylic, polyester.

- Use UV filtering shades on the windows.

- Cover the textiles with UV-blocking plastic: Plexiglas UF3, Lucite AR or Perspex VA.

2 · Artificial Light (For more detailed information about how to properly light textile art, see Part 4 Lighting.)

- All light is harmful to textiles, both natural fibers and man-made fibers.

- Fibers most vulnerable: jute, silk, cotton and linen.

- Colors most vulnerable: dark colors, especially dark blue.

Danger from Incandescent Light

- Hot lights can damage fibers; bright spots of light increase damage and can cause circles of fading where the lights are brightest.

Prevention

- Reduce the brightness with dimmers or with lower wattage lights.

- Move the lights farther away.

- Use "cool" lights and special fixtures that lower the heat projected forward.
  (See page 88, Lighting.)

- Turn on the lights only when people enter the room.

- Put lights outside of display cases, not inside.

- Rotate the artwork.

Danger from High Ultraviolet-Emitting Light

- Ultraviolet (UV) rays are invisible, but very damaging to textiles.

- Artificial light sources high in UV emission: metal-halide lamps and some fluorescent lamps.

Prevention

- Use fibers that have high resistance to UV: glass, acrylic, or polyester.

- Use fluorescent lamps which have low UV emission.

- Put UV shielding around metal-halide lamps.

- If high UV fluorescent light shines on a textile that is otherwise lit by incandescent light, shield the fluorescent light, or add UV shields around the tubes, or cover the fixture with a UV screen.

Storage

- *Before storage, keep textile in a low humidity room for a week at 45% relative humidity, 68 degrees F (20 degrees C).*
- *Pad the folds with acid-free tissue paper.*
- *Wrap the padded textile in unbleached undyed cotton fabric.*

  Caution: Moth balls and crystals repel moths, but do not kill moths or eggs already in the textile. In addition, fumes from moth balls or crystals are unhealthy for humans and animals. Some moth repellents attack dyes and plastic.

- *Seal the wrapped textile in a box made of acid-free cardboard.*
- *Store the box in a cool dry place.*

3 · Excessive Heat

Danger

- Excessive heat breaks down fibers, loosens fibers to cause stretching, causes brittleness, invites nesting of insects, and induces mold and mildew in high humidity.

Prevention

- Do not place textiles above a radiator or heat vent, near hot lights, over a fireplace, or in sunlight.
- Do not store textiles in a hot room or attic.
- Do not put lights inside a display case.
- To prevent lights from getting the textiles too warm:

  Reduce the brightness of the lights.

  Move the lights farther away.

  Use "cool" bulbs in special heat-absorbing or heat-releasing fixtures.

  Turn on the lights only when the textiles are being viewed.

4 · Insects

Danger

- Moths and carpet beetles eat wool, silk, felt, fur and feathers.

Prevention

- Put screens on windows to prevent moths and carpet beetles from flying in.
- Examine all textiles carefully for signs of infestation before putting them in storage or a display area.
- If plants or cut flowers are brought into the room, spray them beforehand with insecticide.
- Do not let plants or flowers touch textiles.
- Protect textiles by careful storage.

Cure for Moth Infestation

- Vacuum away eggs, larvae, etc. (See Vacuuming.)
- Although dry cleaning will kill and remove moths, larvae and eggs, textiles should not be dry cleaned unless absolutely necessary. A professional textile conservator should be consulted, if dry cleaning is required.

Cure for Carpet Beetle Infestation: (Carpet beetles are black, or mottled black and white, about this size: ● .)

- Remove any textiles which are absolutely not infested.
- Inspect remaining textiles for bugs, eggs, larvae or skin casings.

- If infested:

Vacuum the piece front and back.
  (See Vacuuming.)

Consult a textile conservator, who might suggest chemical treatment.

If textile is not treated chemically, maintain periodic inspection. A second vacuuming might be necessary.

Putting the piece in the freezer section of a refrigerator for 72 hours will kill bugs and larvae, but will <u>not</u> destroy the eggs. The eggs can be brushed loose, then vacuumed away with the cold dead bugs.

For very large pieces which are not valuable, take the risk of dry cleaning, which kills and removes bugs, larvae and eggs.

Vacuuming Textiles

Textiles on display, uncovered by glass or plastic, should be vacuumed front and back at least once a year. (Moths lay their eggs on the back side, away from the light.) Periodic vacuuming also prevents dirt and dust from becoming embedded in between the fibers.

The vacuum should be at its lowest setting. Use the upholstery brush attachment to remove dust.

If textile is fragile, or has attachments which could be sucked off, take the textile down and vacuum it through a Fiberglas or Nylon mesh screen laid on top of the textile.

If a fragile textile is vacuumed while it is hanging, put the screening over the nozzle of the vacuum attachment to prevent pieces of fiber from being sucked into the vacuum cleaner.

After vacuuming the textile, also vacuum around the area, then discard the vacuum bag in a tightly sealed plastic bag.

Use of Protective Sprays

The long term effect of protective sprays is not yet known.

What is known is that the chemicals in some sprays break down after many years, get gummy, and therefore hold dust. Textiles that have been sprayed are difficult to dry clean.

The bright side is that most protective sprays <u>do</u> work as advertised.

If a contemporary textile is going to be mounted in a place where it can be touched, ask the artist if it can be sprayed with a grease repellent.

An ethnographic or historic textile should not be sprayed.

---

5 · Dirt and Dust

Danger

- Long neglect of dirt and dust on the textile makes cleaning very difficult.

Prevention

- Keep the room as clean and as dust-free as possible.

- Prevent or discourage people from touching a textile. (Touching leaves skin oils on the textile. Dust particles stick to the oils.)

- Yearly vacuuming prevents dirt and dust from becoming embedded in the fabric.
  (See Vacuuming.)

- Do not wash or dry clean a textile unless it is absolutely necessary. If a valuable piece must be washed or dry cleaned, consult a professional textile conservator.

6 · Mold and Mildew

Danger

- Moisture plus heat set the conditions for the growth of mold and mildew causing discoloration, permanent stains, bad odor and deterioration of fabrics. Darkness and stagnant air speed the growth.

- Especially vulnerable: cotton and linen.

Prevention

- Do not hang or store textiles — framed or unframed — in high humidity places.

- Do not hang textiles directly against a cold outside wall that can condense moisture from a warm room.

- In high humidity climates or spaces, periodically inspect the textiles for discoloration spots, also smell the textiles for the strong sweet odor of mold.

- When framing a textile, the amount of entrapped moisture can be minimized by storing the textile and the framing materials in a low humidity room for a week, then do the actual framing in a low-humidity room, or on a day when the humidity is low.

Stopping Mold and Mildew (Deep stains probably can not be removed.)

- Vacuum the textiles.

- Air-out the textiles in a dry place.

- Use a hair dryer to blow warm air onto the textiles. Set the blower at the lowest heat setting; hold the blower 12 inches (one-third meter) away from the textile.

- If the above treatments do not work, wash or dry clean the textiles following the instructions of a professional textile conservator.

7 · Dryness

Danger

- Dryness causes delicate fibers to crack and unravel.

Prevention

- Do not hang textiles over a heat source.

- Use a humidifier to keep the room between 45-55% relative humidity, at 68 degrees F (20 degrees C), which are the same conditions that are best for wood furnishings.

8 · Fire

Danger

- Fire, smoke, fire-extinguishing agents and water can cause irreparable damage to textiles.

Prevention

- Do not hang textiles where they could possibly blow or fall onto open flame or a hot light, especially a halogen lamp, which gets very hot!
- Use heavy, tightly woven fabrics because flames can wick-up an open weave material (even if the fibers themselves do not support a flame).
- Use fibers which are non-combustible: glass or metal.
- Or use fibers which are slow burning and self-extinguishing, i.e., will stop burning when flame is removed: Nylon, polyester or wool (least flammable of the natural fibers).
- Treat combustible fabrics with fire-retardant chemicals.

Fire-Retardant Treatment

Any fiber can be treated to be flame-retardant, but not all flame-retardant chemicals can withstand cleaning or washing.

For full protection, get certification from the chemical company or the processor that the treatment is "durable" — that it can withstand dry cleaning or washing. If it cannot, it must be treated again after it is washed or cleaned.

Having this documentation in advance will speed acceptance of treated artwork that is to be hung in a public place.

Questions Asked in the Introduction

From School of American Research Collection, Santa Fe, New Mexico

Contemporary Navajo rug – a modern version of an oriental design.

If, in the late 1800's or early 1900's, you had attended a Navajo tribal fair in the Southwest United States, you might have thought that you were in a Persian bazaar! Hung from ceiling beams, draped over railings, spread on the ground were rugs of the same designs as oriental rugs from Turkey or Persia. (Pages 13, 32 and 35 show authentic oriental rugs.)

Your reaction might have been shock, then contempt. Didn't the Navajos have enough initiative to create designs of their own?

But as we now know, the Navajo women **did** weave their own designs (pages vi, 37 and 42). They also borrowed designs from their Mexican neighbors (pages 17 and 57). Their "oriental rugs" were made because the trading post managers and rug dealers gave them pictures of oriental rugs and said, "We can not sell your blankets. But if you put borders around them, we can sell them as rugs – and here are the designs we know people will buy."

The Navajos had endured three centuries of wars, drought, imprisonment and starvation. Yet they survived by creative adaptation to each new challenge. Their weaving and handicraft helped them survive again.

The Navajo rugs that were made for traders in the late 1800's and early 1900's were the best of both worlds: designs accepted in the fine homes of Eastern United States, but still authentic Navajo rugs – tightly woven heavy wool with precise designs using the Navajo colors of black, white, gray, brown and red. Yet each Navajo copy always had some creative modification – a design simplification or even an incongruous addition.

Even today, the Navajos are still adapting and modifying, still weaving and still surviving.

Why do the Amish, known for their plain and somber dress, create quilts so luxuriously detailed and visually powerful?

Living a plain and simple life makes quilt-making a welcomed creative outlet for Amish women.

But it is the <u>kind</u> of life the Amish lead which guarantees that their creative production would be well designed—in balance, in harmony, with purity of line and form.

From the first day Amish children open their eyes, they see perfectly matched chairs, perfectly matched boards on their houses, perfectly stacked bundles of hay in the barn, perfectly fitted (and meticulously sewn) clothing. Disorder or mismatch is painful; self-conscious cleverness is unknown; artiness to attract attention is a violation of Amish morality.

No wonder so many Amish quilts are well designed: the women quiltmakers spent a lifetime surrounded by balance, harmony and pure forms.

These women, working by candlelight on cold winter evenings, cutting and stitching scraps of old clothing, create works of art worthy of any museum—or the walls of the most sophisticated contemporary home. (See cover, bottom, pages 3, 27, 30, 40 and 72.)

Amish "Lone Star" quilt.

From the collection of American Museum of Quilts and Textiles, San Jose, California

"Why is each little design different on a Kuba cloth from Zaire, Africa?"

All the little designs are different on a Kuba cloth because the woman who made it thought to herself, "Within the design motif I have selected, and adding only two colors, how many visually pleasing variations can I create?" In this example, the motif is diamond shaped. Other Kuba motifs are geometric variations of squares, or of weaving patterns.

Starting with a base cloth woven of raffia (palm leaf fiber), she created the design by embroidering or adding cut pile tufting. No advanced drawing or layout is used. The finished cloth will be used as wearing apparel, wall decoration, bridal dowry — or even as currency of exchange.

What contemporary Western designers appreciate is how imaginatively and tastefully these design variations were selected. After all, there is an almost infinite number of ways to break up a diamond shape. And the Kuba restriction of only two or three colors per piece was self-imposed. (Typical colors: black and maroon on tan.)

The discipline of narrowly-limited design options induces intense concentration and high creativity. (Try arranging a pleasing display of fruit using only two apples and three oranges. Or with two apples and only <u>two</u> oranges!) The more restrictive the control conditions, the more that disciplined creativity is required.

Such disciplined creativity can transform a Kuba cloth into high art — stark, dramatic and elegant.

From Marc Leo Felix, Brussels

Kuba cloth.

How did the town of Paisley in Scotland become known as the source for shawls ("paisley shawls") which were originally designed and made in Kashmir, India, and called "cashmere shawls"?

In the 1800's every proper lady owned at least one cashmere shawl.

Not only were these shawls stylish, with their intricate designs in rich colors, but their lightweight wool and fleece blocked out the chill of cold rooms.

Even the hundreds of weavers in India could not keep up with the demand. Women in France, Persia and Scotland set up looms in their homes. Regardless of where they were made, a "cashmere shawl" always included some variation of the basic Kashmir element, the boteh.

The demand for shawls became so great that when Joseph Marie Jacquard invented a machine that wove automatically (the jacquard loom), thirty-six machines were ordered for the town of Paisley, Scotland. By 1820, the town name was synonymous with these machine-made shawls – even though other countries soon after converted their shawl production to mechanical looms. (See page 56.)

But because a machine-made shawl could be made in one day, it cost far less than a hand-woven shawl which took many months to weave.

Now every lady could afford to be stylish and warm – every lady in Europe and even in America. Everyone wanted a paisley shawl! Soon the original cashmere shawl almost disappeared from existence, except for a few very elegant shops.

Today, the original cashmere shawls from Kashmir, India exist only encased in museums or cherished by textile collectors. As time takes its toll, even paisley shawls in good condition are becoming hard to find.

Courtesy of Spink & Son, Ltd, London

Cashmere shawl.

About the Author

Laurence Korwin is a textile artist, collector and consultant.

Slides of his designs are in the libraries of the Cooper-Hewitt Museum, Museum of Fine Arts Boston, Brooklyn Museum, Musée des Arts Décoratifs (Paris) and the Victoria and Albert Museum (London).

To find examples of contemporary and ethno-graphic textiles to illustrate the book, Korwin spent two years inspecting installations and viewing museum and private collections in the United States, Great Britain and Canada.

Korwin is a graduate mechanical engineer (Purdue University); he attended the Art Institute of Chicago and the Institute of Design; he studied batik in Indonesia and sumi-e in Japan.

In Peru he worked with native weavers to develop contemporary designs for their ancient methods of weaving.

He is an ASID allied member and is on the national advisory committee of Arts International.

Photo Credits

Cover
Upper: David Clifton, Chicago
Middle: David Clifton
Back cover: David Clifton

Title Page
Gregory Reich Murphey, Chicago

Acknowledgments
Dick Busher, Dick Busher Photo Graphics, Seattle

Contents Page
Bill Kennedy

Introduction
vi David Clifton
vii Maureen Wikiera, Tom Crane Photographers, Inc.

Selection
5 David Clifton
6 Bill Hedrich, Hedrich Blessing, Chicago
7 Steven Brooke Studios
10 Colin Cuthbert, Crafts magazine no. 63
11 Schecter Lee
12 Bob Hansson
17 Richard Krall
23 Gerald M. Hoffman
28 James Strypek
31 Dennis R. Dodds
39 British Crafts Council
40 Susan Einstein
41 Max Allen
47 Philip de Bay
51 Guy Couture

Framing and Mounting
All photographs by James Strypek, Midwest Photography, Chicago

Positioning
76 David Clifton
77 David Clifton
78 David Clifton

Book Production
Color separations and printing by Total Reproductions, Lincolnwood, Illinois